Where's the Baby King?

A TAMARIND BOOK

ONE NIGHT LONG, LONG AGO, AN ANGEL brought a message to some shepherds on a hillside.

"Good news!" said the angel. "Today the baby King is born in Bethlehem! He is God's son, who has come to save all people. He will bring peace and joy to the world."

A shepherd boy listened in wonder as the angel told the shepherds how they would find the special baby, sleeping in a manger. Then the shepherds hurried off to find him, leaving the boy to look after the sheep.

But the shepherd boy wanted to see this baby King, too.

Early the next morning, the shepherd boy went to Bethlehem, to look for the baby King.

Soon he came to a house.
"Is the baby King here?" he called.

"The angel said he is God's Son," said the shepherd boy. "I must find him."

"I want to see this baby King too," said the man who owned the olive press.

So the shepherd boy and the man who owned the olive press went off to look for him.

Soon they came to another house. "Is the baby King here?" they called.

"The angel said he has come to save
all people," said the shepherd boy. "We
must find him."

"I want to see this baby King too,"
said the carpenter.

So the shepherd boy
and the man who owned the olive press
and the carpenter
all went off to look for him.

Soon they came to another house.
"Is the baby King here?" they called.

"The angel said he will bring peace
and joy to the world," said the shepherd
boy. "We must find him."

"I want to see this baby King too,"
said the spinner.

So the shepherd boy
and the man who owned the olive press
and the carpenter
and the spinner
all went off to look for him.

Soon they came to another house.
"Is the baby King here?" they called.

"The angel said he was born in
Bethlehem," said the shepherd boy.
     "We must find him."
     "I want to see this baby King too,"
said the potter.
So the shepherd boy
and the man who owned the olive press
and the carpenter
and the spinner
and the potter
all went off to look for him.

Soon they came to another house.
"Is the baby King here?" they called.

"The angel said he is lying in a manger," said the shepherd boy. "We must find him."

"I want to see this baby King too," said the shoe-maker.

So the shepherd boy
and the man who owned the olive press
and the carpenter
and the spinner
and the potter
and the shoe-maker
all went off to look for him.

Soon they all came to an inn.
"Is the baby King here?" they called.

"Who is this baby King?" asked the innkeeper's wife.

"God sent an angel to tell us about him," said the shepherd boy.

"He is God's Son," said the man who owned the olive press.

"He has come to save all people," said the carpenter.

"He will bring peace and joy to the world," said the spinner.

"He was born in Bethlehem," said the potter.

"And he is lying in a manger," said the shoe-maker.

"Then let's look in the stable," said the innkeeper's wife. "A baby was born there last night."

So the innkeeper's wife went into the stable with the shepherd boy and the man who owned the olive press and the carpenter and the spinner and the potter and the shoe-maker all following her.

"Is the baby King here?" they called.

The baby was lying in the manger.
His mother, Mary, smiled.
    Then the shepherd boy
and the man who owned the olive press
and the carpenter
and the spinner
and the potter
and the shoe-maker
and the innkeeper's wife
knelt down together to worship Jesus,
God's Son, the baby King.

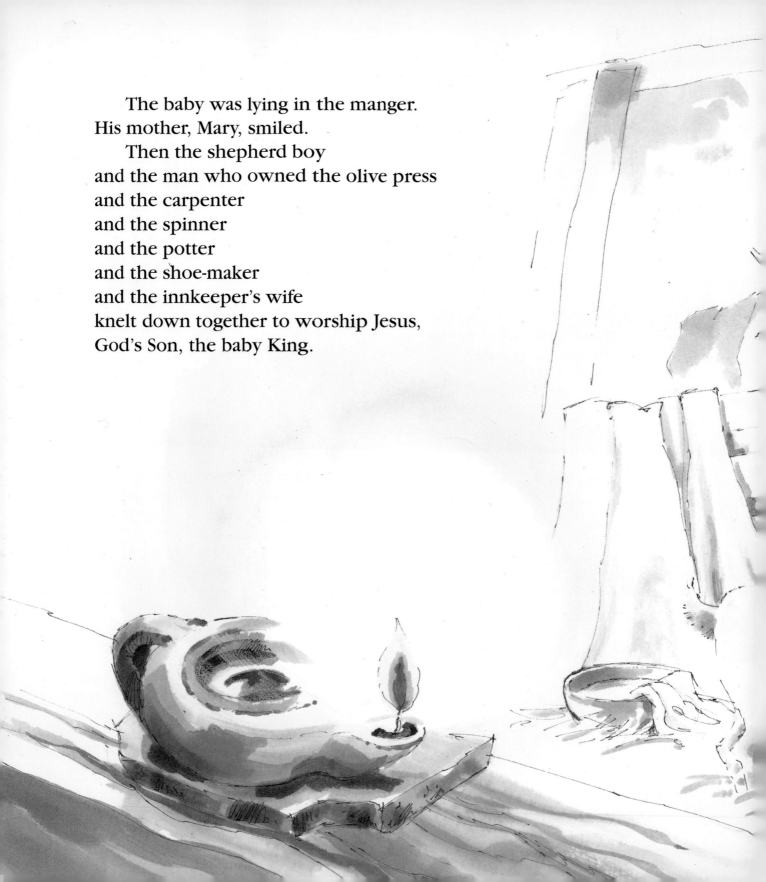

A Tamarind Book
Published in association with SU Publishing
207-209 Queensway, Bletchley, Milton Keynes, Bucks
ISBN 1 873824 18 1

First edition 1996

Printed and bound in China